Usborne
Wipe-Clean

# Halloween Activities

Illustrated by Manola Caprini
Designed by Laura Hammonds
Written by Kirsteen Robson

Use your wipe-clean pen to
do all the activities in this
fun-filled book.

Ethan

# Windy walk

Draw over the dotted lines to finish the leaves.

Connect the numbered dots in order, to finish the spider's web.

Follow the trails to see which tree each squirrel will scamper up.

Draw a line between each pair of matching leaves.

# Pumpkin hunt

Sanchia's friends

Write an X below the wheelbarrow that does not match the others

Use the pen to show Sanchia's friends the way to Sanchia.

Pick a pumpkin

Find and circle 3 squirrels.

Count the pumpkins in each group below, then trace over the numbers.

2   3   5

Draw over the dotted lines to finish the pumpkins.

Sanchia

# Making and baking

Draw over the dotted lines to finish the wings on the costumes.

Spot 3 differences between the two boxes of party decorations.

Find and circle 5 bat decorations.

Count the cookies on each tray,
then trace over the numbers.

Finish the faces
on the pumpkin
lanterns below.

# Party decorations

Find and circle 7 birds.

Follow Rosie's strings to see
which one Jarrod is holding

Rosie

Use the pen to
draw more flags
on the strings.

Jarrod

Draw a line between each matching pair of pumpkin lanterns.

# Getting ready

Spot 3 differences between Max and Mina's monster costumes.

Max

Mina

Connect the sets of numbered dots in order, to finish Ivona's hat.

Ivona

Find and circle 8 striped socks.

Draw over the dotted lines to finish the window frame and curtains.

Draw a line from each hat to the person whose costume needs it.

# Trick or treat

Count the lights on the string below,
then trace over the correct number.

7    8    9

Draw over the dotted lines
below to finish the costumes.

Follow the trails
to see who will go
to each house.

Draw a line between each
matching pair of pirates.

# Pumpkin party

Use the pen to show Scott the way to the pumpkin party.

Scott

Find and circle 7 pumpkin lanterns.

Write an X on the roof of the house below that does not match the others.

Draw over the dotted lines to finish the houses.

HAPPY HALLOWEEN

# Party time

Draw wings on the dangling bats that need them.

Draw over the dotted lines to finish the costumes.

Connect the numbered dots in order, to finish Yuriko's costume.

Yuriko

10
9
8
7
6
1
2
3
4
5

Milly

Molly

Spot 5 differences between Milly and Molly.

# Fun and games

Count the spiders stuck on each web, then trace over the numbers.

8    9    10

Logan

Follow the trails to see who reaches the cauldron and wins the game.

Leo

Draw over the dotted line to show where Amir's ball rolls.

Amir

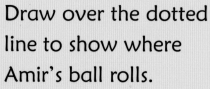